Hummingbird Mode

Lessons from a Latina's Corporate Journey

ALMA LOU GUAJARDO-CROSSLEY

Hummingbird Mode

© Copyright 2024, Alma Lou Guajardo-Crossley
All rights reserved.

No portion of this book may be reproduced by mechanical, photographic, or electronic process; nor may it be stored in a retrieval system, transmitted in any form, or otherwise be copied for public use or private use without written permission of the copyright owner.

It is sold with the understanding that the publisher and the individual author are not engaged in the rendering of psychological, legal, accounting, or other professional advice. The content and views in this book are the sole expression and opinion of the author and not necessarily the views of Fig Factor Media, LLC.

For More Information:
Fig Factor Media | figfactormedia.com

Cover Design by DG Marco Álvarez and Layout by LDG Juan Manuel Serna Rosales
Printed in the United States of America

ISBN: 978-1-952779-40-4
Library of Congress Control Number: 2024902023

Dedication

This book is dedicated to my father, Juan F. Guajardo, who inspired me to do more and to be more throughout his life. His legacy lives on through his children and the hard-earned lessons he shared with us.

Acknowledgments

I would like to acknowledge all the people in life who made me the person I am today and continue to motivate me. I live with gratitude for my family, friends, colleagues, mentors, and young people who prompt me to make a difference in the world. Special shout-outs to Jackie Camacho and Ron Page. Jackie who activated me to write this book, leaving behind a piece of my soul once I am called, and Ron who continues to support and love me through all my phases in life.

Introduction

My journey in corporate America was not an easy one. As a young Latina from a humble background and no exposure to business professionals, I had plenty to learn. My father instilled in me the importance of education and the beauty of a job working with your mind versus manual labor. As a first-generation college graduate, I was determined to make my parents proud. I wanted to live the American dream of a nice car, beautiful home, and enough disposable income to travel and enjoy the various pleasures life has to offer. I was motivated and educated, but not prepared for the corporate culture and the male-dominated industry I was entering. Furthermore, there were very few people who looked like me that I could relate to. I jumped in and landed successfully after overcoming many obstacles. This book is an attempt to share the various lessons I learned on my journey with an easy to remember and stimulating Hummingbird model!

The hummingbird is a magical creature that symbolizes many things across many cultures. Physically, it is the smallest bird in the world, and the only one with the ability to hover, fly upside down, and backwards! Its vibrant colors make it mesmerizing to see as it flaps its wings in a figure-eight pattern, which is the sign of eternity. In pursuit of nectar, hummingbirds energetically jump flower to flower, beating their wings up to eighty times per second! A beautiful and resilient animal that understands the meaning of life.

As my spirit animal, this creature was the perfect specimen to utilize as a model for pursing life's dreams and incorporating my lessons. This book will share my Hummingbird HEARS (Hovering, Energetic, Adaptability, Resilience, Seeking Nectar) model and detail my interpretation and personal examples using powerful "P" words of what it meant to me and how it may help you on your journey. Let's get started! Hummingbird mode "ON"!

SECTION 1

Hovering

The hummingbird's ability to hover in mid-air suggests the appreciation of living in the moment and truly enjoying what life has to offer you from both a personal and business perspective. We need to show gratitude for everything and everyone as we journey our way through life. At times, we are aggravated by ordinary tasks or people and show our frustration. We lose our patience and simply do not perform to our highest standards or react in ways we may not be later proud of. As we "hover" we must be diligent of the PRESENT, have PRIDE in everything we do, and surround ourselves and show appreciation for the PEOPLE in our lives. Let's examine each of these "P" words more closely.

Present

The importance of being present and living in the moment. We must value and appreciate all the moments we have in life, given we do not know what the next second will bring or who will still be with us. Take advantage of opportunities and pause to celebrate. Spend time with the person you love, get a cup of coffee with the person you met at a conference, listen to the person sharing a story with you. Stay focused and productive at work so you can clearly appreciate your time later. As you get older life goes only faster and you will never have the time again. A life with regrets is one that is not lived. As someone who appreciates travel and experiencing cultures different than mine, I am so pleased I took the adventures I wanted when I was younger (even if it meant working longer hours, going by myself, or holding off on a new washing machine). As I become less agile and slower, I recall moments like hiking Camel Mountain, walking ruins in Greece, and appreciating the sun rise behind Taj Mahal. Experiences create moments. Often in our youth we get caught up in material items and lose the true essence of what really matters in life. Act fast and seize what is important to you. You create your own happiness and living in the moment ensures some of it will happen.

Pride

Pride in who you are and what you do is essential in building your confidence and showcasing your abilities to others. You should never be embarrassed of who you are or where you came from. Your background or obstacles in life simply reflect your strength and provide you tools for continued success.

Many things define me. I am proud to be a Latina and bilingual. I am proud to be educated and humbly raised by parents who loved me and instilled in me a strong work ethic, my faith in God, and the courage to achieve anything I set my mind to. Given circumstances in their homes, neither one of my parents attended college, and only my mother received a GED from high school; but they inspired me to pursue an education and to do my best in whatever job I was given. Your work reflects who you are and should be done with pride, even if it is scrubbing the floor.

I am proud of my heritage and my family made it easy for me to be my authentic self, even when it was not so easy. I now know that your authenticity is the catalyst for change—and that you should never be afraid of who you are—you have something to offer and to teach others. As a person with a different cultural background, sexual identity, etc., you bring a different dimension and enlightening perspective to the table that is unmatched and beyond your talent, education, or business experience. No one sees the world quite like you. Your viewpoint is the differentiator that inspires innovation. Let your voice be heard. Say it loud and be proud!

People

You must have the presence of mind to be aware of the people entering your life and surrounding you. Someone you meet at a networking event could have a lasting impact in your life; but you must acknowledge and engage the moment the interaction occurs. It is critical to find people who respect you and will stand up for you when you are not in the room. People who will believe in you and understand the value of what you bring and what you stand for. People in my life have defended, advocated, and promoted me, and they included people from the highest corner office to those sweeping the floor. Find your people and mentors early in life and continue to collect them throughout your career and life's journey. Most people want to help and are flattered to be asked.

The right people are also crucial in your private life. Remember to honor and respect the people in your life like your parents, grandparents, or any relative or special person who has guided and supported you. Gratitude is essential and we often do not realize how much they have provided until later in life.

Find others who will encourage you and back you. People who will build you up, not break you down. People who will bring value in your life and not distract from it. People who will share your dreams and chase them with you. Take a close look at your current circle and make the right choices to move forward. Life is simply too short to be weighed down by negativity. These choices are often very difficult and painful, but once made create a freedom and lightness you may have never felt before. I personally went through a divorce and ended a long-term friendship because of the effect it was having on me. I was drained of energy and unhappy but not wanting to give up on my commitments as a friend and spouse. However, at times we must do what is best for us to continue the positive momentum. Make the choices that are right for you. As Oprah Winfrey said, "You have to be in the driver's seat of your life because if you are not, life will drive you."

SECTION 2

Energetic Lifestyles

The hummingbird's boundless energy is readily apparent as it hovers and zips from flower to flower in search of its nectar. Its constant movement and tireless flapping remind us to chase our goals. We must be PASSIONATE, PRODUCTIVE with PURPOSE, and stay POSITIVE as life happens. Our dreams do not come true by sitting still! Let's jump into the nectar of what each of these powerful "P" words have to offer.

Passion

Passion, as defined by Dictionary.com, is "any powerful or compelling emotion or feeling." To feel passionate about something is an amazing gift and can propel you to accomplish things you have only dreamed about. Passion is where you live in your heart.

It should be acted upon before the fire in your belly subsides. Your feelings will inspire you to keep your momentum and will satiate your inner self. How many times have we watched the clock while doing something you have no passion for, or could not listen to someone speaking when you had no interest or passion for the topic? You must learn to recognize these feelings and pursue those objects in life that you have an optimistic passion for. Passion applies to all your pursuits in life and can be the catalyst that allows you to live the life you want to lead.

Earlier in this book, I indicated I was a first-generation college graduate from a humble background. I recall working with my family trying to figure out how to pay tuition as I was passionate about an education. My father words still ring in my mind of the value of working with your mind versus your hands or hard labor.

My brother mentioned an engineering co-op school that the program covered about 90 percent of the tuition. However, I was not particularly passionate about engineering. But upon further investigation, I discovered there was a degree that matched my interests and passion: management systems with a major in marketing. My desire for education and the ability to research options and receive guidance from mentors helped me to achieve my educational dreams.

It was not an easy journey. Leaving your family, surrounded by strangers, trying to adjust to new friends, social pressures, etc. However, my passion for education and making my family proud inspired me to move forward. Now as a retired executive, my appetite is to serve our youth. Teaching lessons learned to help them accelerate their success in life's journey!

Productivity with Purpose

The hummingbird's constant movement reminds us to always be moving with purpose in mind. In pursuit of our life goals, we must act with thoughtful intent and self-reflection. Is what I am doing today helping me with my life's vision or goals? Am I giving 100 percent to this activity, and is it a true reflection of my capabilities? Understanding at times we must move faster than we like given time or other constraints, but will you be proud of your accomplishment? Is it a true reflection of who you are and the work you are capable of?

In my career journey, there were often many times I was not the best spoken, most political, or best dressed person in the work group. However, my work results and productivity spoke louder than all my self-perceived faults. I always worked with a purpose or end-goal in mind. I can recall working late and learning everything about my product to ensure I could sell the value and benefits to my clients with the end goal of winning the sales contest and earning the recognition. I wanted to be known for being knowledgeable and delivering results. I also always raised my hand to do the extra work or take on the extra responsibilities to show my value and that I was not afraid to work hard. Moving targets are harder to hit, and if you are always moving you will always end up somewhere. Productivity with purpose is a winning combination and can help you achieve your goals faster than you anticipated. Always keep in mind what you are doing and what you are trying to achieve whether from a business or personal perspective. If you believe it, you can achieve it, and having a purpose behind productivity will bring that vison to life!

Positivity

What you project to the world often comes to fruition. I recommend reading the book, *The Secret* by Rhonde Byrne, if you have not done so already. The whole premise is that positive energy attracts positive things in your life. I have always been the girl with the cup half full (versus empty) and can honestly say it has worked well for me. Any disappointments in life always have a silver lining or a lesson that can be learned that will serve you later in life. We should maintain a positive outlook and push forward.

    Have you ever noticed how good you feel when someone smiles at you? Having a positive attitude is so critical in achieving your dreams. Life is not always easy and often provides us with valuable lessons or heartaches that only help us to grow as individuals. You must have a positive frame of mind if you want to endure in the long-run and ultimately finish the race. Working with people with positive dispositions makes people more productive, happier, and easier to be around. People are naturally attracted and are more willing to help people that have a smile on their face and a positive outlook. Having a positive attitude will also inspire you to take risks in life that could be very rewarding! I recall being afraid to take a job across the country away from my parents and siblings but decided to take a positive attitude. I self-reflected about the new experiences I would have, the promotion I could earn, the new people I would meet, and the possibility of family visiting me! It turned out to be an amazing experience! This new opportunity afforded me the chance to do many other things with my family that I would not have had the chance to if I had not taken the job or been positive about the opportunity. POSITIVITY PAYS BACK!

SECTION 3

Adaptability

The hummingbird has the natural ability to quickly change the direction it is flying in to meet its needs. This is an exceptional talent and one that must be practiced and fine-tuned by people. Life is very unexpected, and we find ourselves needing to adapt. Whether it is getting a new boss, going off to school in a different city, obtaining a new job, welcoming a baby or having a parent move in with you, you find yourself needing to adjust. Your response and willingness to be open and accepting to change is critical to success. In my personal journey I learned the following lessons that I have distilled down to the "P" words of PERSONALLY, PROFESSIONALISM, and PAST. Let's dive in!

Personally

Perhaps my most hard-earned and best lesson in my life was to never take anything personally! My skin has grown exceedingly thick over the years, but it was a long journey. I truly wished someone had shared this lesson with me earlier as it would have saved me plenty of personal anguish.

I cannot tell you how many times I have been looked at "funny," screamed at, been cut off on the highway, or been told something offensive by someone. Life is tough, you never know what the other person has experienced throughout the day, how they have been raised, or what they have been exposed to in life that creates that "bad" moment for you.

We must keep in mind that America is a melting pot of many people with varying cultures, experiences, education, etc. Diversity in the United States is amazing but can cause hurtful experiences if you allow yourself to be personally offended by every ignorant or rash comment made. My experience has taught me that many people simply are not aware they are being offensive, and I have learned to take the high road by creating a teaching moment if possible. Calling people out in a friendly manner can be a real eye-opener and have a lasting impact. To date, when I have chosen to have the conversation, it has always gone well, and each party has learned something new. I have educated people on various topics including different ethnic cultures, the LGBTQ+ community, religion, and even how to ask questions if they are not familiar with something. Sure, there are times when people mean to be cruel and offensive, but these people are not worth our time.

The world is full of people and experiences that we will never be able to fully encounter. However, learning to adapt and to stay open will enrich your life and expand your knowledge. Choose to see offensive remarks as an opportunity to teach or simply accept people's ignorance (growing thick skin!). Life is a much easier ride if we respond accordingly and never take anything too personally, especially if they are people you barely know or are not invested in.

Professionalism

The definition from the Cambridge Dictionary for professionalism is "the qualities connected with trained and skilled people" but adding more significantly the definition of presence, "a person's ability to make his or her character known to others," we begin to understand what is truly vital in our career journey. Our actions and appearance are of the utmost importance.

Let's start with your physical appearance. One should always be aware of the accepted dress culture of your chosen career path and/or the company you are joining. As a young professional in a first-time job, you always should lean conservative until you have a full understanding of what is acceptable. A dark professional suit or dress and being well-groomed should be the standard until you have established yourself and your capabilities. Once you are in good standing you can adapt to the culture of the company or organization. I recall wearing a red dress with ruffles in one of my first meetings in corporate America! I was an eighteen-year-old intern with no understanding of what was acceptable in the business world. Entering a room full of men with dark blue business suits left me feeling very uncomfortable and anxious and I would not wish this on any young person. Confidence is critical in your early years and ensuring you are appropriately attired and not feeling out of place will help build your self-assurance. Your physical presence is your first impression, and you should always lead with your best foot forward with a clear understanding of what is appropriate. Do not be afraid to ask questions. You will learn to adapt to the culture and add your personal flare once the timing is right.

Understanding the behavioral norms and adapting to them is extremely important as well. However, you must not be afraid to have a voice and have a presence. For instance, for some managers being on time at a meeting is showing up 5 minutes early. This is where you may hear and learn about items outside the meeting agenda you would not know otherwise. Paying attention is critical, and adapting your behavior to make you more effective in your role is critical. I recall learning how some presenters did not like questions regarding their presentations until after they have finished. I realized many of the questions you have may be answered throughout their presentation, and this ultimately saves the presenter time. I had to adjust my behavior as my curiosity would sometimes have me raising my hand to ask a question, until I learned the norm. Professionalism and presence are interpreted in many ways depending on the world you are entering. You must be aware and learn to adapt to what is acceptable to ensure you are successful in your journey.

Past

There are many lessons to be learned from the past, whether from your own experiences or that of others. We should proceed through life collecting the many flowers planted in the field of knowledge to seed in our own personal garden. History should be respected and referenced, with the understanding that we will also be open to change. Life is an evolution that often brings new innovations and perspectives that will create positive transformations. Being respectful and understanding the value of history, while adapting and accepting new ideas, will bring transcendental change.

> *"Life can only be understood backwards; but it must be lived forwards."*
> **-Søren Kierkegaard**

From my personal experience, I found tremendous value in researching the past work of others as well as interviewing experienced colleagues before creating the change I wanted to see for a project. This not only provided me with some key foundational knowledge but also helped secure support from the folks that I engaged as changes were being made. Part of our aspirations as humans is to leave a legacy in our lifetime. The past is a legacy of those who came before us. Their footprints and the impact they made are crucial lessons we must learn from to move forward in the next generation. It is key to realize a person's legacy is much broader than the material items they leave behind. We must keep in mind our own personal legacies, via the words we say, the words we write, or any actions or creations we take or make. Whether good or bad, you may be leaving a legacy. What do you want yours to be?

SECTION 4

Resilience

The hummingbird is known for its resiliency given its ability to endure long arduous migrations. It is tiny and mighty! Its surprising strength, tenacity, and determination reminds us of what we all might be capable of if we believe in ourselves. It provides inspiration and aligns with my personal "P" words of PERSEVERANCE and PRAYERS.

Perseverance

Perseverance is about not giving up! No matter how difficult, how long, or how far out of reach something feels, perseverance will keep you going. Like the hummingbird we continue with tenacity and determination until we reach our destination. Most people have experienced all types of difficulties while chasing life goals, including financials, language barriers, leaving family behind, housing, or simply not having access. However, their drive and determination pulled them through! It is never easy and many of you will experience failures along the way. Remember that we cannot control what happens at times, but we can certainly control our reaction, which is everything. Hold your head high with dignity, take a pensive moment, and develop a purpose driven plan to succeed. It has been said, "Failure is simply the opportunity to begin again, but this time more intelligently."

Over my life's journey, I have encountered many obstacles, including people who tried to discredit me, lack of knowledge or experience, or not having enough money for school, clothes, or even food at times. However, I refused to allow these difficulties to create my destiny. I worked harder, researched, asked questions or sought advice, and created a network of people and organizations who were willing to help and support me. I was not afraid or ashamed to ask for help. Many of these people and organizations remain in my life today and have proven to be good friends who I returned favors to. No matter how dark it seems there is always a place to turn. Keep trying and keep asking, you will persevere!

Prayers

As we go through difficult times, we all need a higher self or power to turn to and ask for support and or guidance. Not all of us have family and friends, or at times we are simply by ourselves on our journey. Having faith or beliefs that ground you so you know you are never alone is extremely helpful. As a Christian, I list prayers, but know there are so many other beliefs and religions to consider. No matter where you are in the world, countless spiritual communities exist that are willing to support you. Having faith in a higher power should provide you with the strength you need to continue down your path. Moments of meditation or simply connecting with nature also can regenerate your soul. Take the time to self-reflect and wish for the best for you and others. Faith can provide the foundation and be the rejuvenating pool you need when you are feeling alone or in need of help.

I found tremendous comfort in the church when I was transferred to another state for a job opportunity. I had left family and friends behind and did not know a single person in my new location. The local church provided me with a sense of community and helped me to re-center myself in what was important in my life. I value my relationship with God and have endless gratitude for the many blessings in my life. Understand where you spiritually connect and what will help guide you through life's journey. Today, I find my favorite church is in my heart, where I pray every night expressing my gratitude and requesting guidance for my daily trials.

SECTION 5

Seeking Life's Nectar

The hummingbird's primary source of food is the nectar of flowers. Given the energy they expend, the hummingbird will visit hundreds of flowers a day, often consuming three times their body weight a day in nectar! Ask yourself, what is my sweet nectar in life? How actively do I pursue it? Throughout the years, I have found my sweet nectar to be centered around the following "P" words of PAY IT FORWARD, PERSONAL LIFE, and POTENTIAL. Let's visit each of these flowers in my garden of life.

Pay it Forward

Please remember who you are and where you came from, no matter how successful you become. There is no place for ego. If you want to continue to grow you must do what's right in your heart and soul. We need to be willing to help others as others have helped us. In many communities, there is no question how we help and support our families, but we should extend beyond and offer support to people we do not even know. Being a secret angel with no recognition or exposure of what you have done to help is especially fulfilling. Take the time to volunteer, mentor, and give back to the communities we work and live in. The smallest things can make a huge difference in someone's life. Seeing a small child's face light up with a special gift, handing a few dollars to a homeless person, or volunteering to support an elderly person clean their home will help you earn your wings!

One of my favorite sayings is, "Whatever you give to life, it gives back to you. Do not hate anybody. The hatred which comes out from you will someday come back to you. Love others. And love will come back to you." I have found this to be true so many times in my life. The more you give, the more life blesses you. Nurture your soul by being a servant leader and supporting those around you.

Personal Life

Be ready to run! As we enter adulthood you will find life to be very busy and you will run! For instance, you may: Go to school, go to work, find a relationship, buy a home, buy a vehicle, travel, have a family, have friends, have children, and have pets. You will have fun and you will cry. You will have energy and you will be tired. You will run out of time! Life is so filled and so precious and so short. You need to balance and understand your priorities in life to ensure nothing is compromised that you truly value. How important is the big house versus spending time with people you love?

Take the time to understand what fills your cup and that of your partner in life. You will need to have a full tank to be able to address all the demands in life you will encounter. I highly recommend you read *The 5 Love Languages: The Secret to Love That Lasts* by Gary Chapman. This book will help you to understand and better relate to your partner or the people in your life that support you. It is also critically important you take care of yourself. Take the time you personally need to stay healthy and have a good frame of mind. This could mean exercising, spa treatments, reading a book, taking a trip, or maybe even spending time alone. To keep running, we need to take care of ourselves! Your personal life at the end of the day is what keeps you inspired and happy!

Potential

The world unfolds to your potential and the potential of all the possibilities around you. Be aware and keep your eyes open to the endless opportunities that the world offers you. The biggest regret comes from the chances we have missed in life. Potential can be viewed in so many different ways, from utilizing the talents you have to the missed opportunities that others offer. Self-reflect as to what you may have already missed in life and lean into the potential of all the possibilities that are currently surrounding you. The potential of spending time with loved ones, the potential of learning something new, getting an education, or pursuing a creative idea that came to you. Do not be afraid to take the leap or invest the time into a dream that can bring you happiness. The short time we have in life should not be taken for granted. We all have special talents and offer a different perspective in life. Understand your talents and abilities and live to the potential of the gifts you have been given in life. You have the potential to leave your mark on the world. Believe in the power of you and what you can do!

    Thank you for taking the time to read this book and hope you found some valuable insights. Everyone's journey in life is different but lessons we learn may help others along in theirs. My wish is this book inspires further conversations and connections.

ABOUT THE AUTHOR

Alma Lou Guajardo-Crossley, who recently retired after a thirty-eight-year career with General Motors (GM), is now leveraging her wealth of experience to mentor the next generation of leaders, particularly young Latinos launching their careers. This, together with her commitment to education, integrity, perseverance, and servant leadership continues to shape corporate America and the Hispanic/Latino community.

During her tenure at GM, Alma Lou held many leadership positions, guiding and mentoring emerging talents. Notably, she played a pivotal role in launching the GM Global Diversity COE in 2011 and served as the director of Corporate Diversity and the Global Employee Resource Group (ERG) Network until her retirement. Alma's mission was to strategically position GM as a global example of inclusivity.

Championing diversity, equity, and inclusion, Alma Lou oversaw the GM Global ERG Network, supporting over 50,000 employees in fostering a sense of community and belonging. A Michigan native, she earned her undergraduate degree from GMI in 1990 and her master of business administration from the University of Phoenix in 1997.

Throughout her career, Alma Lou motivated teams, consulted for dealership operations, and implemented impactful marketing programs, contributing significantly to GM's success. Committed to her Hispanic heritage, she received numerous accolades, including being named one of the 100 Most Influential Hispanics by Hispanic Business in 2011 and culminating in 2023 with the BRAVA Award from LATINO Magazine.

Residing in Houghton Lake, Michigan, with her longtime partner and pets, Alma Lou's legacy extends beyond her remarkable corporate journey to her influential role in fostering diversity and leadership.